Newbridge Discovery Links®

WHAT A JOB!

Becky Gold

Newbridge

A Haights Cross Communications Company

What A Job!
ISBN: 1-58273-726-6

Program Author: Dr. Brenda Parkes, Literacy Expert
Content Reviewer: Evangelos Dousmanis, Instructor, Photography
  and Computer Graphics, Binghamton University, Binghamton, NY
Teacher Reviewer: Lisa Donmoyer, Talbot County Schools, Easton, MD

Written by Becky Gold
Editorial and Design Assistance by Curriculum Concepts

Newbridge Educational Publishing
333 East 38th Street, New York, NY 10016
www.newbridgeonline.com

Cover Photograph: A photographer on location in the mountains
Table of Contents Photograph: A beautiful pattern in a diatom

Cover: Bobby Model/National Geographic Image Collection; Contents page: Darlyne A. Murawski/
National Geographic Image Collection; page 4: Cheo García; page 5: CD cover for "Michael
Gregory/Red," photo by Cheo García; page 6: Dream sequence from "Pick a Pet" by Cheo García and
Shelly Rotner, published by Orchard Books, 1999; page 7: Cheo García; page 8: Peter
Brueggeman/© 2001 Norbert Wu/www.norbertwu.com; pages 9–10: © 2001 Norbert Wu/
www.norbertwu.com; page 11: (top) © 2001 Norbert Wu/www.norbertwu.com, (bottom) Stuart
Westmorland/Mo Young Productions/www.norbertwu.com; pages 12–13: ©2001 Norbert Wu/
www.norbertwu.com; page 14: National Geographic Image Collection; pages 15–17: Darlyne A.
Murawski/National Geographic Image Collection; page 18: William L. Allen/National Geographic Image
Collection; pages 18–21: Annie Griffiths Belt/National Geographic Image Collection; page 22: Gavriel
Jecan/Art Wolfe, Inc.; pages 23–26: Art Wolfe/Art Wolfe, Inc.; page 27: (top) Art Wolfe/Art Wolfe, Inc.,
(bottom) Gavriel Jecan/Art Wolfe, Inc.; page 28: Amy Crews; pages 28–29: Collage by Nina Crews from
"I'll Catch the Moon" © 1998, published by Greenwillow Books, a division of HarperCollins Publishers;
page 30: Collage by Nina Crews © 2000, from "We the People," published by Greenwillow Books, a
division of HarperCollins Publishers; page 31: Darlyne A. Murawski/National Geographic Image
Collection

10 9 8 7 6 5 4 3 2

TABLE OF CONTENTS

It's a Snap: José Ramón García 4

Going to Extremes: Norbert Wu 8

Tiny Wonders: Darlyne Murawski 14

Faraway Places: Annie Griffiths Belt 18

Wild About Wildlife: Art Wolfe 22

Over the Moon: Nina Crews 28

Glossary 31

Index 32

Websites 32

IT'S A SNAP

JOSÉ RAMÓN GARCÍA

José Ramón García at work in his studio

A good photo can inspire, teach, and spark new ideas. And it takes hard work and special skills to take a good photo. Professional photographers work in many different situations, from high-tech studios, to ballparks, to wilderness areas, and even scientific laboratories. Every different situation may require a different kind of equipment, and each photographer must be prepared for the unique challenges that a photo session may bring.

Have you ever had your portrait taken by a photographer at school? The photographer brings in special lights and sometimes a background setting for your picture. Then it's up to you to look into the camera and smile. But what if you don't want to smile? Or if you forgot to comb your hair? Or if you blink at the wrong moment? Then the photographer must be patient.

Why do you think José chose a red background for this portrait of a guitarist?

When it comes to photography, José says, "Everything is a fiction," as can be seen in this fanciful photo in which a girl imagines many kinds of pets.

José Ramón García knows a lot about that. He's a professional who has photographed thousands of people.

José says that when he started taking pictures, he shot everything—from buds on trees, to rocks and flowers. After he became a **commercial photographer**, he discovered that he best liked **portraiture**: taking pictures of people.

José often works in his studio, where he has lights, backdrops, and a setting in which people feel at home. Before he takes a portrait photo, he has a conversation with the subjects to get to know them and help them relax. He takes "mental images" of the subjects' expressions, how they sit and move, how they hold their hands and gesture. In this way he can best capture each person's uniqueness when he begins to shoot the film.

José also does photography to create advertisements. Sometimes he takes his own photos for ads. He also uses other people's photographs to create new images, combining different elements on a computer. Using special computer software, he can work with the images to make some incredibly interesting new photographic art.

José used a special kind of paper to add warm tones to this black-and-white print.

GOING TO EXTREMES

NORBERT WU

Norbert Wu with the equipment he uses to take underwater photos in Antarctica

Norbert Wu is one of the best-known underwater photographers in the world. He has been diving for about 25 years. And his assignments have taken him from icy Antarctica to tropical Borneo. Norbert's work requires a lot of special gear. The cameras he uses need to be protected from the water. They are surrounded by large casings that can weigh up to 100 pounds and are difficult to move around underwater.

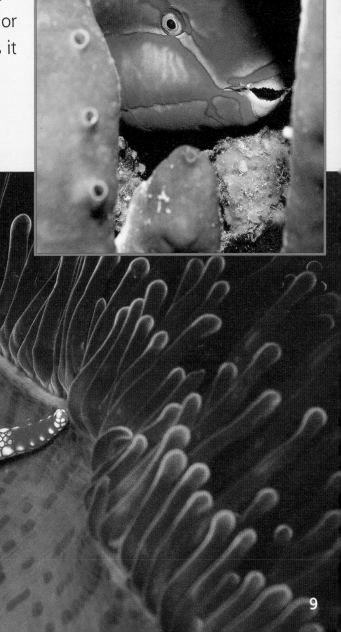

Photography can be slow work. Just setting up a shot—without snapping any pictures—can take almost an hour, sometimes longer. The ocean water itself challenges even the most experienced photographer. Whether the photographer is diving or on a boat, the water's motion makes it difficult to hold a camera steady.

Norbert photographed this parrot fish and starfish in a coral reef near the island of Borneo.

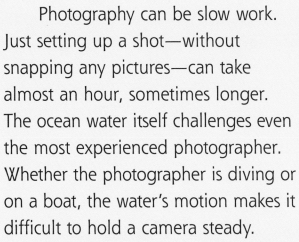

As a child, Norbert was always interested in marine life. By second grade, when he saw Jacques Cousteau, a famous marine biologist, on television, he was totally hooked on the watery world. Later on, in high school, Norbert learned to dive. His first dives were in Georgia's Lake Lanier, where he saw only "a muddy bottom, a catfish, and some golf balls."

Some people think that great photographers are born, not made. Not Norbert. "It's baloney," he says. "Anyone can do it. You can train the eye. I just happen to work full-time at it."

Made of thousands of tiny stainless-steel rings linked together, this "suit of armor" can protect against smaller sharks such as the blue shark, but not against large ones like tiger sharks and great whites.

Norbert snapped this fierce Weddell seal (above) under the Antarctic ice. The giant octopus (right) was found in the ocean off the Pacific Northwest. Notice how big it is compared to the diver!

Anyone might be able to learn to take photographs, but not everyone is as excited about sharing the water with sharks as Norbert is. To handle this challenge, he wears a custom-made, chain-mail suit which weighs 20 pounds over his wet suit. To control how deep he goes underwater, Norbert must also wear a **buoyancy compensator (BC)**, an inflatable vest. This goes on over the chain mail. If a shark were to take a bite out of the BC, Norbert would sink to the bottom of the sea.

Photographing underwater takes stamina—especially in the subfreezing waters off Antarctica. While most people can barely stay in for an hour, Norbert has made numerous 90-minute dives—in a row!—to photograph a colony of Weddell seals in the Antarctic.

Norbert has photographed endangered coral reefs in many parts of the world. Corals get sick easily, and even die, because of pollution or the carelessness of divers who touch or break them. Norbert takes special care while swimming and moving heavy camera equipment near the reefs.

It may seem like a long way from catfish and golf balls to sharks, seals, and reefs—but not if you have the determination and the will of Norbert Wu.

These fish are spawning (laying eggs) in Australia's Great Barrier Reef.

This fish, a six-foot-long giant wrasse, patrols the seas near the Great Barrier Reef.

TiNY WONDERS

DARLYNE MURAWSKI

Darlyne Murawski prepares a specimen to be photographed under a high-powered microscope.

Darlyne Murawski is a photographer who is also an artist and a biologist. She takes photographs of tiny organisms—a job which allows her to use both of these skills. As a scientific researcher and photojournalist, she has photographed insects, bacteria, and **diatoms**, all too small to be seen without a microscope! She has also taken many photos of larger insects and butterflies. Darlyne travels around the world to collect her exotic specimens. Sometimes she takes

This common bedbug almost appears to be smiling.
It was magnified so that it looks 90 times larger than it is in real life.

pictures of them while they are alive. But microscopic
photography often involves killing an insect. She places her
specimen between two pieces of clear glass, making it very
flat, so that its details can be seen clearly. The glass—called a
slide—allows her to see all the way through the specimen.
Then she places the prepared slide under the microscope, which
contains a built-in camera. Next she **focuses** her **lenses**, and
then snaps her pictures.

Darlyne has spent a lot of time photographing diatoms—the tiny, shell-like structures that are actually certain kinds of algae. Diatoms are so tiny that about 25 million of them would fit in a teaspoon! To photograph diatoms, Darlyne uses cutting-edge microscopes with extremely high magnification. In this way she captures amazing, magical images of these almost invisible life-forms.

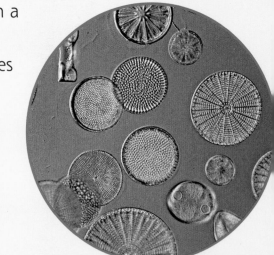

Notice how the shapes of these diatoms are like flowers or wheels.

What do these
diatoms remind you of?

FARAWAY PLACES

ANNIE GRIFFITHS BELT

Annie and Don Belt, shown here with their guide, rode camels to reach Petra. They wore Bedouin headdresses to protect against the sun and wind.

Annie Griffiths Belt and her husband Don, a writer, have traveled all over the world searching for stories and pictures of amazing places and the people who live in them. One of those places is an ancient city in the Middle Eastern country of Jordan, called Petra.

A man rests on a red sandstone ledge outside the ancient city of Petra.

Annie began her career as a newspaper photographer while she was still in college. She has written about and photographed all kinds of interesting places, including the desert in Baja California and the beautiful coastline near Vancouver, Canada. Her photographs frequently appear in magazines such as *National Geographic*.

The red sandstone cliffs around Petra bear traces of the ancient city, and provide a colorful subject for Annie.

Finding the right **perspective** is an important part of any photographer's work, but especially a **photojournalist**'s. Look at the photo on page 18. It is taken straight on, as a close-up: The people and the camel fill the frame. This is not an accident. The photographer wants us to focus on the faces, to get a sense of the personalities of the people—and perhaps even the camel! Now look at Annie's large photo on page 21. It has a different perspective. It was taken from above, to give the viewer a bird's-eye view. This photo shows us the place more than the people. Annie uses this perspective to convey a sense of what a mysterious and amazing place Petra is.

Petra is full of surprises. This beautiful floor was discovered by archaeologists exploring an ancient church.

Bedouins—native people of the Jordanian desert—watch from a high ledge as tourists admire the structure called *Al Khazneh*.

WiLD ABOUT WiLDLiFE

ART WOLFE

Art Wolfe up-close with two of his subjects: king penguins and seals in South Georgia Island. He uses a tripod to keep his camera steady while taking pictures.

Art Wolfe is not only a photographer. He is also a wildlife conservationist. He is committed to capturing the world's fast-disappearing wildlife on film for future generations. Art has been a professional photographer for over 25 years. He may have been inspired in his work by his parents, who were both artists. Art has worked on hundreds of locations. Each year, he is on the road for more than nine months, and shoots more than 2,000 rolls of film!

Art often uses a **telephoto lens** to take pictures of wild animals. This long lens, which attaches onto a camera's built-in lens, allows him to get a close-up shot of an animal that would be dangerous to go near. The lens works a little like a telescope, and makes the image he is photographing appear much closer than it actually is.

Most photographers working outdoors shoot their pictures with natural light. When photos are taken in a studio, the light can be controlled. But outdoor photography requires that

Art used a telephoto lens to safely shoot this close-up picture of a mother polar bear and her cubs.

the photographer carefully measure the light and adjust equipment as the light changes. Just imagine how different the light is when the sun is shining bright in the sky, and is then covered by a passing cloud. Before he takes a picture, Art uses a small instrument called a **light meter** to measure the light. Then he adjusts his camera to get the shot he is after. If there isn't as much light as he would like, he can hold his camera's shutter down for several moments, allowing more light to reach the film inside the camera, to produce a lighter, brighter image.

Notice the different colors of these stars. The fixed star at the extreme right is the North Star.

Art's skill with lighting is seen in the beautiful sunset colors and golden glow on the coat of the camel in this photo.

The way a photographer uses his or her camera can change the way we see things. For example, the photo of the starry night sky on page 24 was taken with a very long **exposure**. Art kept his camera's **shutter** open for many hours, so that he could capture the light of the stars on film while the earth rotated. This is not the way we normally see stars; the photo tells us something interesting about our relationship to the night sky.

Look at this close-up shot of a mother and baby gorilla. We see a little bit of the forest in this photo, but the focus is on the gorillas. Why do you think Art might have chosen this arrangement?

Notice the interesting, graceful pattern of these alpine ibexes' curved horns. Art traveled to the Swiss Alps to photograph the ibexes (above and below).

A lot of thought goes into setting up each shot. The way things are arranged, called the **composition** of a shot, affects the way we see it, and the story it has to tell. A photographer seeks to balance the different elements in his or her composition.

OVER THE MOON

NINA CREWS

Nina Crews has been taking pictures since she was very young.

Nina Crews is a photographer who uses her images to illustrate the children's books that she also writes. She has always been inspired by the skyscrapers, the people, and the neighborhoods of New York City, her hometown. These elements are found in many of the books that she writes and illustrates for children.

Nina always loved art, and when she reached college, she became serious about photography. She also discovered **collage**, a technique that allows her to cut up images and create new pictures, layering images over one another. "Collage allows me to use photography playfully and to tell a story on many levels," she says. This is just one more example of the creative way in which photographers use their skills to express their own vision as artists and storytellers.

Nina admits that people do not always think of her as a photographer. "But," she explains, "there are as many different kinds of photographers as there are different ways of seeing."

In this illustration, Nina took separate photos of the girl climbing the ladder, city buildings, and the moon. Then she cut up the photos and put them together to create this imaginary scene.

All photographers learn how to use a camera, to understand different types of film, and to compose a shot. But each photographer also needs skills for his or her own area of expertise. That might mean knowing how to scuba dive or mountain-climb. Or it might mean learning to use computer programs, or new artistic techniques. Every photographer wants the same thing: to create a picture that tells a story. The difference is that every photographer uses his or her unique skills and interests to help get the job done.

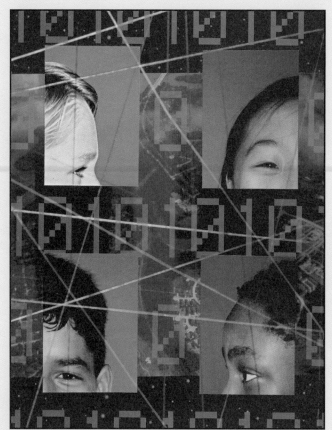

Nina created this collage to accompany a poem about moving into the 21st century, where computers are becoming a more and more important force in everyday life.

GLOSSARY

buoyancy compensator (BC): a device that helps a diver stay afloat at a particular depth in water when weighed down by heavy equipment

collage: a method of combining images to achieve an artistic effect

commercial photographer: a photographer who creates images for advertising

composition: the arrangement of elements in a photograph

diatoms: tiny shell-like structures that are kinds of algae; they are too small to be seen in detail without a microscope.

exposure: the effect of light on the film

focuses: sharpens the appearance of an image by adjusting its distance from the lens

lenses: pieces of glass shaped to direct light rays into a camera so they can be recorded on the film

light meter: an instrument that measures the amount of light that is available

perspective: the viewpoint from which a photographer takes a picture

photojournalist: a person who takes pictures and uses them to tell stories, especially news stories

portraiture: formal posed photography of people

shutter: a part of the camera that regulates the amount of time during which light is allowed to strike the film

telephoto lens: a camera lens that makes faraway objects appear closer than they actually are

INDEX

alpine ibexes 27

Antarctica 8, 11

bedbug 15

Bedouins 18–19, 21

Belt, Annie Griffiths 18–21

Belt, Don 18

Borneo 8–9

buoyancy compensator (BC) 11

camels 18, 20, 25

cameras 8, 9, 15, 23, 24, 25, 30

collage 28–30

composition 27

Cousteau, Jacques 10

Crews, Nina 28–30

diatoms 14, 16–17

film 7, 22, 25, 30

García, José Ramón 4–7

giant wrasse 13

gorillas 26

Great Barrier Reef, Australia 12–13

king penguins 22

lighting 23, 24

microscopic photography 14–17

Murawski, Darlyne 14–17

North Star 24

octopus 11

parrot fish 9

Petra, Jordan 18–21

perspective 20

polar bears 23

portraiture 4–7

sharks 10–11

starfish 9

telephoto lens 23

underwater photography 8–13

Weddell seals 11, 12

wildlife photography 22–27

Wolfe, Art 22–27

Wu, Norbert 8–13

WEBSITES

Here are some Websites worth visiting:

www.artwolfe.com

www.norbertwu.com

www.nationalgeographic.com